This book is
your passport
into time.

Can you survive
in the
Ice Age?
Turn the page
to find out.

D0951527

DONATED BY

The Flock Family

Bantam Books in the Time Machine Series
Ask your bookseller for the books you have missed

TIME MACHINE 7

Ice Age Explorer

by Dougal Dixon
illustrated by Doug Henderson
and Alex Nino

A Byron Preiss Book

BANTAM BOOKS
TORONTO • NEW YORK • LONDON • SYDNEY • AUCKLAND

RL 5, IL age 10 and up

ICE AGE EXPLORER
A Bantam Book/June 1985

Special thanks to Ann Hodgman, Anne Greenberg,
Martha Cameron and Ruth Ashby.

Book design by Alex Jay
Cover painting by William Stout
Cover design by Alex Jay
Mechanicals by Studio J
Typesetting by David E. Seham Associates, Inc.

Associate editor: Ann Weil

"Time Machine" is a trademark of
Byron Preiss Visual Publications, Inc.

ISBN 0-553-24722-0

Published simultaneously in the United States and Canada

Bantam Books are published by Bantam Books, Inc. Its trademark, consisting of the words "Bantam Books" and the portrayal
of a rooster, is Registered in the U.S. Patent and Trademark
Office and in other countries. Marca Registrada, Bantam Books,
Inc., 666 Fifth Avenue, New York, New York 10103.

PRINTED IN THE UNITED STATES OF AMERICA

0 9 8 7 6 5 4 3 2 1

ATTENTION
TIME TRAVELER!

This book is your time machine. Do not read it through from beginning to end. In a moment you will receive a mission, a special task that will take you to another time period. As you face the dangers of history, the Time Machine often will give you options of where to go or what to do.

This book also contains a Data Bank to tell you about the age you are going to visit. You can use this Data Bank to help you make your choices. Or you can take your chances without reading it. It is up to you to decide.

In the back of this book is a Data File. It contains hints to help you if you are not sure what choice to make. The following symbol appears next to any choices for which there is a hint in the Data File.

To complete your mission as quickly as possible, you may wish to use the Data Bank and the Data File together.

There is one correct end to this Time Machine mission. You must reach it or risk being stranded in time!

THE FOUR RULES
OF TIME TRAVEL

As you begin your mission, you must observe the following rules. Time Travelers who do not follow these rules risk being stranded in time.

1.
You must not kill any person or animal.

2.
You must not try to change history. Do not leave anything from the future in the past.

3.
You must not take anybody when you jump in time. Avoid disappearing in a way that scares people or makes them suspicious.

4.
You must follow instructions given to you by the Time Machine. You must choose from the options given to you by the Time Machine.

YOUR MISSION

Your mission is to travel back to the Ice Age and identify a mysterious animal that our Ice Age ancestors painted on a cave wall long before the dawn of history.

This animal has a spotted coat and a long horn on its head. It looks just like a unicorn. Strangely, it is found among pictures of recognizable animals, including bison, horses, and reindeer, while other nearby caves carry pictures of mammoth and woolly rhinoceros.

Could Ice Age people have seen an animal that today's scientists do not know about?

Your mission is twofold. First, you must see how primitive people first expressed their artistic ability and watch how Ice Age art developed. Second, you must travel the world to study the animal life of the time and see what creatures Ice Age people painted. As you search to identify the paintings and the painters, you will face ferocious beasts, hostile early cultures, and the bitterest climate that the earth has ever known.

 To activate the Time Machine, turn the page.

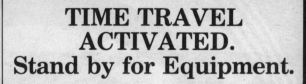

**TIME TRAVEL
ACTIVATED.
Stand by for Equipment.**

EQUIPMENT

For your mission into the Ice Age, you will need the best cold-weather clothing available. This includes thermal underwear, woolen sweater, waterproof pants, an insulated wind-proof parka, and sturdy boots. Your backpack will also contain a flashlight, which will be essential since you will be spending some time in caves.

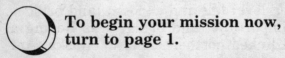

To begin your mission now, turn to page 1.

To learn more about the time to which you will be traveling, go on to the next page.

DATA BANK

1) The Great Ice Age—the Pleistocene Epoch of the Quaternary Period—began about 1.6 million years ago and ended only about 10,000 years ago.

2) Ice formed and melted repeatedly during the Great Ice Age, splitting the Ice Age into cold "glacial advances" separated by warm "interglacials," in which the climate may have been warmer than it is now.

3) Throughout earth's history there have been other ice ages, most notably in the Precambrian, Devonian, and Permian periods.

4) Ice didn't cover the whole globe during a glacial advance. It spread from the poles, squeezing the earth's zones of temperate and tropical climates together toward the equator.

5) Because of the water locked in the ice, the sea level fell and exposed land bridges. One important land bridge was Beringia, which linked northern Asia to Alaska. Animals could move from one continent to another across this dry land during glacial advances. So could people.

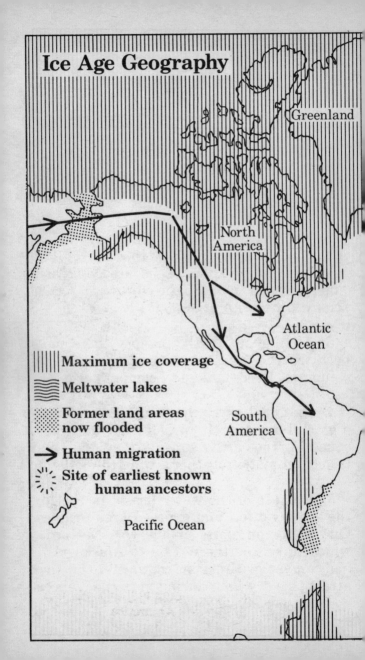

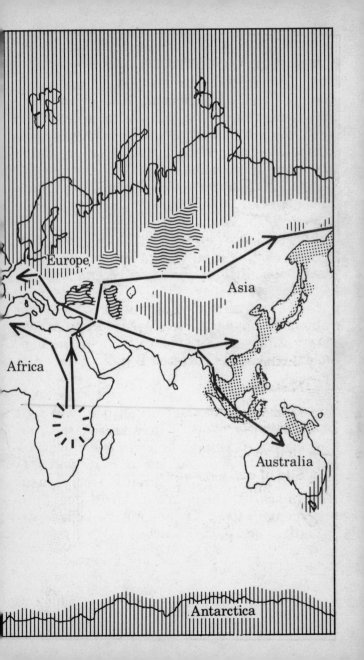

6) During the interglacials, animals particularly well-adapted to the cold followed the retreating ice, while warm-climate animals could move from around the equator into more temperate areas. Especially in Europe, where there was a great change in temperature, the animals of the interglacials differed from those of the glacial advances.

7) The Ice Age may not have ended yet. Earth's climate is still very variable, and there have been "little ice ages" in recent times.

8) As you travel back to the Great Ice Age, remember that time is measured by approximating how many years ago an event took place. This is abbreviated B.P. for before the present.

9) Throughout your adventure, you will encounter our evolutionary ancestors, from the apelike *Australopithecus* to *Homo sapiens neanderthalensis,* a subgroup of our own species, *Homo sapiens*. Be careful. Though usually peaceful, these groups are sometimes suspicious of strangers and may be hostile, especially when food is scarce.

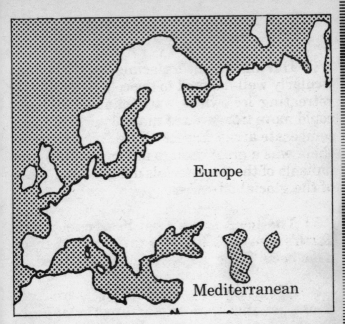

Wildlife in Europe
during the glacial advances:

A) The woolly mammoth, a shaggy-coated elephant with huge tusks. (Large animals tend to evolve in cold climates.)

B) The woolly rhinoceros. Unlike its modern African counterpart, the woolly rhinoceros was well-adapted for life in a cold climate.

C) The cave bear, a giant plant-eater of uncertain temper.

D) The Irish elk, a deer with a 10-foot antler span.

E) The mountain goat. Its range was more widespread than that of mountain goats today.

Wildlife in Europe
during interglacials:

A) The *Palaeoloxodon,* a straight-tusked elephant.

B) The auroch, a wild ox.

C) The cave lion, the biggest cat known to science.

Wildlife in the Mediterranean:

A) The pygmy elephant, only three feet high.

B) The pygmy hippopotamus.

C) The giant rat, as big as a cat.

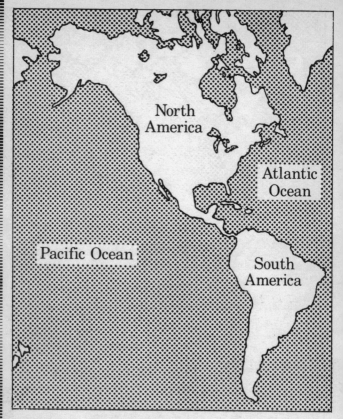

Wildlife in North America:

A) The mastodon, a shaggy, long-tusked elephant.

B) The saber-toothed cat, with teeth huge enough to kill thick-skinned prey such as mastodons.

C) The horse, which evolved on the continent, then moved to Asia via the land bridge.

D) The giant condor, a bird of prey.

Wildlife in South America:

A) The giant ground sloth.

B) The *Glyptodon*, a giant armadillo.

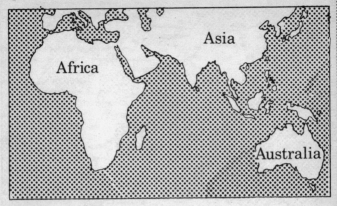

Wildlife in Africa:

A) The *Sivatherium,* a giant giraffe with a short neck and mooselike horns.

B) The *Moropus,* relative of the horse, but with claws instead of hooves.

C) The giant hyena.

Wildlife in Australia:

A) The *Procoptodon,* a giant kangaroo. (Kangaroos are marsupials, which are found almost exclusively in Australia. Marsupials carry their young in pouches.)

B) The *Diprotodon,* a rhinoceros-sized wombat.

C) The *Thylacynus,* the marsupial version of a wolf.

DATA BANK COMPLETED. TURN THE PAGE TO BEGIN YOUR MISSION.

 Don't forget, when you see this symbol, you can check the Data File in the back of the book for a hint.

You are in a woodland glade, beneath the shade of a mighty oak tree. Golden sunlight slants down through the boughs of the surrounding trees, illuminating swarms of insects that dance and buzz in the still air. Long grasses grow around your knees, and a huge beetle hums past your head and flies heavily down toward a row of alder trees that lines the bank of a still, lily-covered pond.

You realize something must be wrong.

You are supposed to be in an ice age, yet the heat inside your parka is rapidly becoming unbearable, and your woolen clothing is beginning to itch against your skin. The flies and mosquitoes from the pond are gathering around, attracted by the sweat on your face.

Maybe you're in the wrong time period altogether. Should you stay where you are or jump in time?

 Jump back in time 200 million years. Turn to page 14.

 Jump forward in time 800,000 years. Turn to page 7.

 Stay where you are. Turn to page 8.

You should have been prepared for the biting cold that now cuts through your clothing and threatens to freeze your flesh. Frantically you tear into your backpack for your warm clothes. You struggle into your parka, pull the drawstring of the hood around your face, and plunge your numbed fingers deep into your sleeves.

Now that the immediate danger of freezing has passed, you can look around. You're standing on a crag in a howling blizzard. Snow conceals most of the landscape, but below the black rocks on which you stand, you can see the jagged whiteness of a glacier. The whirling snow slackens for a moment, and now you can see right across the icy surface.

It is an ice sheet, like the pictures of Antarctica you have seen. Its surface is striped by rocky debris carried away from the mountains you see in the distance. About a mile away, a crag—smaller than the one you're standing on—juts up above the whiteness. The glacier is moving imperceptibly past this crag, splitting and reuniting behind it.

The swirling whiteness of the blizzard closes in once more, and you can see nothing else.

The cold is now penetrating your parka. You are no closer to finding the cave paintings or the people who painted them. But your immediate need is just to survive. And to do that, you must get out of this bitter cold. You could jump to modern times and see what this landscape is now like, or you could go back to a warm interglacial to take the chill out of your bones.

 Jump south to warm up. Turn to page 20.

 Jump to modern times. Turn to page 11.

You stand by a frozen river, a snowy landscape with stark leafless trees spreading away on all sides. This looks more like an ice age. Now your expedition can really start.

You set off toward a wood along the riverbank, but a strange noise meets your ears. It sounds like people laughing and singing and having a good time.

In an ice age?

You round a bend in the river and come upon an amazing sight. Dozens of tents and huts have been built on the ice, and gaily colored flags are streaming from them. Coaches and wagons are drawn up along the bank, their horses lazily munching at heaps of straw laid out for them. Hundreds of people are sliding and skating on the ice. A band plays an assortment of strange instruments. And in the middle of it all, on a kind of wooden raft, an ox is roasting on a spit above a fire. A huge ice carnival is in progress.

You have jumped forward to the seventeenth century, one of the "little ice ages" of historical times. Not what you're looking for!

Jump back 800,000 years.
Turn to page 8.

ou remove your parka and sweater and, with your backpack over your arm, you step out from beneath the oak tree and into the sunlight. You hear a splashing noise from the direction of the pond and stroll down toward the stands of alders and willows. There's a large animal wading there.

Wouldn't it be amazing, you think, if that animal turned out to be the unicorn creature you're looking for?

You reach a bed of bulrushes, and your boots sink with a squelch into the mud of the water's edge. Now you can see across the pond. The animal is only an elephant, knee-deep in the water, its back toward you, feeding on water weed. You turn to go, but the elephant wades out into deeper water. Now you see its head for the first time. You are amazed. It's not like any elephant you have ever seen. Its tusks are long and straight and reach down to below the water surface. Each ivory column is twice as long as you are!

Now you have it! The straight-tusked elephant was one of the animals of the interglacials—the warm periods of the Ice Age that came between the retreat of one ice sheet and the advance of the next. You haven't missed the Ice Age after all—you've just dropped into one of its particularly warm spells. You suspect that this is an interglacial period and that you are about 800,000 years before modern times. This should be the time of the most advanced *Homo erectus*, the human ancestor that came just before *Homo sapiens*.

It would be fun to see what our ancestors are doing at this time. The most famous fossils of *Homo erectus* were found near Peking. That means going to China.

Jump to China, now! Turn to page 16.

ou are still on your crag, but the weather is much warmer. Below you, instead of the glacier, there stretches a city. It's a very dirty city, with smoke from thousands of chimneys forming a thick sooty haze that hangs everywhere.

Then you notice the other crag, the one that was splitting the glacier. There's a castle perched on it now, and on one side of the rock there is a gentle slope. It is as if the glacier, moving past, had scraped out the hollows at each side and piled up its rocky debris in the lee of the crag.

Now you know where you are—you recognize the castle. This is Edinburgh, Scotland's capital. That explains the smoke as well; nineteenth-century Edinburgh used to be known as Auld Reekie, which means Old Smoky, because of it.

You remove your parka and walk down the hill toward the city. Soon you come across a group of men in frock coats and top hats who are looking carefully at the rocks in a cutting by the side of the road.

"Good morning," you say to a man at the edge of the group.

"Aye, mornin'," says the other, in an accent that is strange to you. "And a guid queer mornin' it is too. First all these havers about ice, and now a young loon like yersel' turnin' up dressed like that!"

"Havers"? What does he mean? And what did he say about ice? You think that this may be important. "What's happening here?" you ask the man.

"See that man in the big hat?" he replies. "His name is Jean Louis Agassiz. He's a professor from Switzerland. He says that yon marks on the rock were caused by ice sliding past. He says there must have been glaciers here a long time ago. It's all havers! Those marks were put there by the Lord's flood."

You know better. You have just seen the glaciers that made these marks. However, you have no intention of arguing with the man. There's a newspaper sticking out of his pocket. You can just see the date: 1840.

You realize, with excitement, what a historic moment you have stumbled upon. This is the first time anyone had an inkling that an Ice Age had actually occurred!

You say good-bye and walk on. You look at the scratches on the rock yourself. You suppose that if anyone had told you that they had been caused by ice, especially on a warm day like this, you'd say "havers" too. But with the knowledge that you have, you can see that it is true. The glaciers were so powerful that they scraped away the hollows in which the city is built and carved the strange shapes of the hills around it.

You're learning a lot about the Ice Age, but you've still got to find the prehistoric people who may have painted caves.

Jump back 20,000 years in time to North America. Turn to page 36.

Your boots sink into soft mud. You have landed in a shallow stream of icy water. The plain around you is crisscrossed by thousands of such streams, all flowing from the sparkling white edge of an ice sheet about three miles away. This must be the glacier outwash plain, carrying away the water thawed from the ice and spreading out the glacier's rocky debris in the form of sand, gravel, and mud.

Along some of the larger heaps of soil there are fringes of green, where plants are growing. You squelch across to the nearest of these for a closer look. You are surprised at what you find. You had expected to see reeds or heather or lichens. Instead you find a compact ferny growth like nothing you've ever seen.

Suddenly a very strange animal darts out of the undergrowth, startled by your approach. It stops and gives you a cold stare. It's like a lizard, about two feet long, but its limbs are held beneath it like a dog and it's covered with hair instead of scales. It's like a cross between a mammal and a reptile. In fact, it's a mammallike reptile!

The animal scampers off out of sight, leaving you shocked at what you have just seen. Mammallike reptiles lived in the Permian Period.

You are in the wrong ice age!

 Jump ahead 200 million years. Turn to page 8.

Smoke swirls around you, choking your nostrils and squeezing shut your eyes. Heat sears your face and your bare hands. You hear nothing but the roar and crackle of flames. This isn't what you expected of an ice age!

It must be a forest fire. And you are in the middle of it!

You panic and run blindly, staggering up a grassy slope, smoke and streamers of soot drifting up after you. Presently you find yourself on a rocky outcrop. For the moment you're safe.

A few yards away, on another outcrop, stands a group of about ten naked figures. They are about your height and look almost human, which surprises you. You had expected *Homo erectus* to be much more apelike. The face, however, does remind you of a chimpanzee, with a mouth that juts out, no chin, heavy eyebrows, and no forehead. You are actually looking at your own ancestors!

However, they don't see you. A few of them are picking berries from a nearby bush, eating

some and putting the rest in a pile. Most of them are staring down the hill toward the fire. Suddenly they begin to jump up and down, jabbering excitedly. It's not exactly speech, but they are communicating their emotions to one another. What they're excited about is that the hunters are returning. A group of about seven men is winding its way up the grassy slope between the limestone outcrops. Two carry the charred remains of some animal between them, a victim of the forest fire. Another—a very distinctive man with hair lighter than the rest—carries a burning branch. He runs ahead to show it to the rest of the tribe.

At first they're afraid, looking from the branch to the destruction of the forest below, but the light-haired man tries to calm them. He shows them how it works, setting fire to some dry grass.

Meanwhile the rest are tasting the charred flesh of the dead animal. They seem surprised at how easily it pulls to pieces and how easy it is to chew. The whole tribe gathers around and begins to pull the carcass apart.

Not everyone is so fascinated by this new food, though. A child looks up from the group and sees you on your rock. It has never seen anything like you before! With a puzzled look on its chimpanzee face, the child crawls through the grass toward you.

But while its elders are having their first taste of cooked meat, they aren't noticing what is happening to the little fire that they started. It's becoming a big fire! The dry grass of the slope is flaring up, and a wall of flame is sweeping down to where the child is toddling toward you. It stops dead at the sight and begins to scream.

You jump down, pushing through the grass to rescue the child of one of your ancestors. You reach the little figure just before the flames do and gather it up, whimpering, in your arms. With the smoke swirling around you again and the flames reaching for your legs, you struggle back to your rock and place the child at a safe height.

But as you are clambering up as well, you lose your footing and tumble down into the grass once more. The fire is almost upon you! You must jump. To a time after the fire has burned itself out.

Jump ahead ten years. Turn to page 28.

ou are standing in long grass. A rolling yellow plain sweeps down toward a broad lake, still and quiet beneath a tropical sun. Beyond the lake a gentle-sided volcano reaches up, smoke pluming from the top. Here and there on the plain, umbrella-shaped thorn trees stand in their pools of shadow.

The place is so obviously Africa that you expect to see herds of zebra and wildebeest winding their way down to the lake. Instead you see a number of animals that are quite unknown to you. There's one like a short-necked giraffe with moose's horns—*Sivatherium*.

A huge horse strolls by, but you don't pay it much attention until it rears on its hind legs by a thorn tree. Then you see that it has no hooves! Instead its feet are equipped with huge claws, which it's using to tear down leafy branches. This beast is *Moropus*. Strange things exist here, 1.6 million years ago.

However, there is a group of animals that you do recognize: chimpanzees. But they are very tall chimpanzees, and they're walking with a very upright stance.

With a shock you realize that these are *Australopithecus,* one of our apelike ancestors. They haven't noticed you; they're busily picking berries among the thorn bushes.

The *Australopithecus* look up and come toward you screeching and showing their teeth.

You turn to run—and are struck on the shoulder by a stone. Wincing in pain, you struggle through the long grasses until, with a shock, you are brought up against another group of people.

These are different, though. They are smaller and less menacing-looking. They're a completely different species of *Australopithecus.* Unfortunately, they are no less hostile. They leap about, screaming and waving their arms.

The first group catches up with you, and immediately there is a great battle between groups. They scream and yell at each other and throw stones and sticks. You lie facedown in the grass and hope that all this passes you by.

Eventually it does. The heavy australopithecines, which you now recognize as *Australopithecus robustus,* go back to their berry bushes, and the lighter form scamper down toward the lake.

You watch them go, and see them chase some very large hyenas away from their kill. Then they gather around the dead animal and begin to feed. These smaller forms, *Austral-*

opithecus africanus, are evidently meat eaters, and they can work together to steal meat from other animals.

The sky is getting darker every moment, and the sulfurous smells and the fine ash from the grumbling volcano are making things very uncomfortable.

 Jump forward 1 million years. Turn to page 34.

A great gray shape looms over you. You step nimbly out of the way just as it crashes past. It's an elephant. There is another just behind it, and two more at each side. You've landed in the middle of an elephant stampede! Which way to run? To the side? With the flow? Or should you stand still?

You stand your ground, and soon the last of them has passed. With relief you look around you. Now you can see what was causing the stampede. The grassy slopes of the valley in which you have landed are ablaze. Dozens of figures—*Homo erectus* again, as far as you can make out—are running down the valley waving burning sticks, driving the elephants before them. You turn to see where the elephant herd has gone, and you find them in trouble. They've blundered into a bog and are floundering about in the mud, trumpeting in panic.

Then about fifty figures emerge from hiding. Armed with rocks and spears, they set upon

the trapped animals, killing them where they struggle. Most of the elephants free themselves and escape, but eventually three lie dead in the mud and shallow water. The hunters leap and shriek in jubilation.

You are disappointed. You thought that you had seen the discovery of fire in China. Now here in Spain *Homo erectus* is using fire as well. You realize that fire was not a single invention; it must have been discovered several times and used by people all over the world.

Now they are cutting up the dead animals with stone blades and cooking the meat on a number of fires. After the cooked meat is distributed, the great hunting party splits up into small groups, which wander away in different directions.

The men you have seen must belong to many different groups that have come together just to tackle this elephant herd. They must have expected the herd to migrate through this valley at just this time and planned their attack beforehand.

This is the kind of cooperation you would expect of modern humans. But you are amazed to see it here, 800,000 years ago! You think to yourself that early humans could not have been as "civilized" as this. You're becoming curious about the early stages of human evolution. You could go back to the very beginning of the Pleistocene to see just what our ancestors were, or you could jump forward in time to try to follow humanity's later development.

Jump to Africa in the beginning of the Pleistocene Epoch, 1.6 million years ago. Turn to page 20.

Jump farther north to 20,000 B.P. Turn to page 4.

ou're standing in the same place. It's early evening, and for a moment you wonder if you have merely moved ahead a few hours. Then you notice that the forest in the valley has begun to grow again, with vigorous saplings surrounding the few charred trunks still standing. There is no sign of the grass fire on the hillside.

Nor does there seem to be any sign of *Homo erectus*. Then, from farther up the slope, a flickering light catches your eye. You leave the shadow of the rock and climb the slope to investigate.

The light is coming from a cave. Inside the cave is the *Homo erectus* group, and they have a fire going at the entrance. It is a properly constructed and cared-for fire, with stones built around it to prevent it from spreading and pieces of meat—skewered by sticks— roasting over it. The people are huddling around it for its light and warmth. They have come to accept fire as a friend.

There is a noise behind you. You turn to see a young man standing behind you. There is something familiar about his face, and he seems to recognize you. Of course, you think. This is the child that you saved!

With a flash of inspiration you wonder if he can help you in your quest. Groping about on the ground, you find a charred stick, the remains of a previous fire. You use it as a pencil and draw the unicorn animal on the rock surface. If he can recognize it, he might be able to show you where such an animal lives. The young man looks at it, looks at you, and then back at the drawing. It is no good. He has no idea what you are doing. Drawing is totally unknown to him. It will be tens of thousands of years before any sort of art develops. But at least his tribe has mastered the use of fire.

The young man runs toward the main group. The man with light hair stands up to welcome him. Then you notice that the older man has horribly disfiguring scars up his arms and legs. They have learned to use fire, but the learning has been difficult and painful.

So far, you've not seen any cave paintings, though.

You could jump to Spain, where *Homo erectus* remains have been found, or jump forward in time.

 Jump to Spain. Turn to page 24.

 Jump 800,000 years forward in time. Turn to page 7.

You're on a tundra landscape. Away to one side, tiny in the vast flatness, is an encampment with a fire burning. A small group is heading across the chill plain toward it. Some of them are pulling a kind of sleigh, with a dead caribou upon it.

You trudge through the hummocky tussocks of wiry grass to greet them. These are obviously specimens of *Homo sapiens*—modern human beings. This is the place geologists call Beringia.

These people you see now are very likely the ancestors of American Indians, migrating across from Asia at least 20,000 years before modern times.

You're quite close to them now. You raise your hand and shout "Hi!"

You are shocked by their reaction! The men turn and grab their weapons. Now they're throwing bone-tipped spears and running at you with antler-headed axes. You turn and run.

You try to figure out their reaction. These are hunter-gatherer people. The food on a

tundra landscape such as this must be very scarce. Any newcomer must be seen as a possible competitor for this food. This is not like the situation with *Homo erectus* in Spain. There was plenty of food there—in the form of elephants—and all the *Homo erectus* hunters could combine to hunt them.

Now you wonder what to do. You could stay and defend yourself. Or you could jump somewhere else—there may be more animals to the south.

 Stay and fight. Turn to page 40.

 Hide behind a large grass tussock and jump to the south. Turn to page 44.

You are in the same spot. The volcano is quiet now and the lake has shrunk to a mere water hole, but the rest of the landscape looks much as it did. The weather, however, is much, much cooler.

You can now see two groups of apelike animals. The first is still foraging for berries and looks much like a gorilla. This must be *Australopithecus boisei,* relative of the larger australopithecine that you saw earlier. The other is smaller and more upright, looking something like *Homo erectus.* You think that this must be the descendant of the smaller meat-eating australopithecine. Indeed, two members of the group are carrying a dead antelope between them. As this group passes the berry-picking group, the two groups ignore each other completely. They've evidently evolved in such different directions that they don't compete with one another anymore.

Then you notice that the smaller ones are carrying stones with them, and these stones have been chipped to give sharp edges. These are the first tools! The creatures you are looking at must be *Homo habilis*—the first tool makers!

This is exciting, but you're not progressing in your quest. You are a long way from finding out what the cave-painted unicorn really is. And anyway, you haven't tasted the real Ice Age yet, have you?

Jump forward in time to 20,000 B.P. Turn to page 4.

You are in North America, standing in a tundra landscape. The weather here is cold, and you must find some warmth.

A little way away there is a kind of encampment. There are several huts and a big fire. That's for you, you think. Running, so as not to get chilled, you reach the fire—but there's no one here! Still, this gives you time to warm up.

Warmed by the fire, you become drowsy. Your head drops forward onto your chest.

Suddenly you are awake. You can hear voices. A group of human beings—these are obviously human beings, despite their thick swaddling of animal skins—are coming into the camp. By the looks of their baskets full of plants, they've been out gathering food.

They put down their baskets close to one of the huts. Then, still chattering to one another, they take up pots and leave the camp again, presumably to fetch water. That was close! They didn't notice you.

You are hungry after your sleep, and those

baskets look tempting. Cautiously you walk over to them. They contain blue-colored berries and some kind of grass seed. You are not sure if you will like these, but gingerly you try a berry. Delicious! Greedily you take another, then another. Soon the basket is half empty.

A shout comes from behind you. You swing around. A very angry woman stands there, waving a stick, and others are crowding round behind her.

You'd better go! But you would still like to know more about this place and these people.

You run round the back of the nearest hut and jump a mile away.

 Turn to page 31.

ou are standing on another plain, this time in South America. Horses graze near you. Giant sloths browse among the scattered trees. Mastodons in a herd string out toward the hills. You catch a glimpse of a saber-toothed cat slinking among the grasses.

Something is wrong. Have you jumped anywhere at all? You could be in the same place, with the collection of mammals you see around you here. At this stage of the Ice Age, two continents, North and South America, must be joined, so that the animals can move freely between them.

You don't seem to be much nearer your goal. You have not seen an animal that looks anything like your unicorn—either here or in North America. In fact, none of the animals you have seen, except for the horses, appears on the cave wall with the unicorn. You could try another time and see if the correct collection of animals crops up. Or you could try another continent altogether.

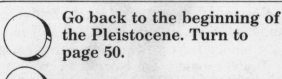

Go back to the beginning of the Pleistocene. Turn to page 50.

Try somewhere else. Go to Australia. Turn to page 54.

You stop in your tracks and swing around. All you wanted to do was to make friends!

You seize a bone-tipped spear that has stuck in the ground and swing it like a club at the first man who approaches. It catches him across his forearm. He yells and drops his antler ax. He won't be using that arm again for a while.

The rest of the group of human beings gathers around you. Now they're really angry. It's time you were off.

You duck down and run, shouldering your attackers out of the way. The squelchy mud and the stiff grass tussocks keep you from running very fast, but as you look behind you see that the others are not following. They have all turned to help their injured companion, and they're paying no attention to you.

You suspect that you are on the wrong track. These people seem to be too busy just staying alive to develop any sort of art. You could jump forward in time to see if anything develops in this area. Or you could jump to the present day to see if modern studies shed any light on your search.

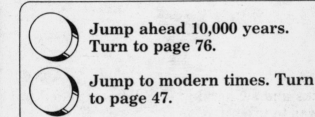

Jump ahead 10,000 years. Turn to page 76.

Jump to modern times. Turn to page 47.

ou stand still and hold your breath in pure terror. The saber-toothed cat comes closer and closer—but stalks right by you!

You let out your breath in a burst of astonishment and relief. Then you remember. Saber-tooths eat elephants and other large animals. That's what their long teeth are for. They can inflict deep wounds on thick-skinned prey, rather than kill with a quick bite to the neck as do other cats. They are just not interested in small stuff like yourself.

This one slinks off in the direction of the mastodon herd, lowering itself into the grass as it goes.

Suddenly you hear a great splashing noise. One of the giant sloths you saw earlier has stumbled into the tar. It's thrashing around in panic, but the more it struggles, the more firmly it is trapped.

The saber-tooth has noticed this too. Abandoning all thought of the mastodon herd, it turns and runs to the mired sloth.

You know very well what is about to happen, but you can't prevent it. The saber-tooth leaps on the trapped sloth. But it slips, and slides down the sloth's shaggy flank into the tar. Now both prey and predator are hopelessly stuck.

You look around you. There are all kinds of interesting animals here, but none that looks at all like the one you seek. Where to go next?

 Jump to South America.
Turn to page 39.

 Jump farther inland in North America. Turn to page 100.

I t's still 20,000 B.P., but the climate is warmer. It should be—you have moved to California. You see mountains to the east, but you are standing on a gentle plain that slopes gradually toward the Pacific Ocean, which you can see between hills in the west. You're on the site of what will someday be Los Angeles.

Here and there you see pools of water, but there is a strange air of death about the place. Huge bones are sticking out of the water, and the branches of the few scattered trees are weighed down by vultures.

These are the Rancho La Brea tar pits. Pettroleum has oozed out of the rocks and hardened into a sticky goo on the surface. Rainwater lies in puddles on this goo, and unwary animals have become trapped in it.

What kind of animals, you wonder? You look around. A herd of horses moves across the plain. A few hundred yards away, in a grove of trees, there is an animal as big as an elephant, but it is covered with hair and has no trunk. To your surprise, it raises itself on its hind legs and thick tail and starts pulling at the branches. It's a giant ground sloth!

The sloth's tugging disturbs a flock of vul-

tures, and they flap off across the plain, screeching and cawing. They settle in a tree about half a mile away and watch the passage of a group of elephants. These elephants are very long and low in profile and have shaggy coats and long tusks. You recognize them as mastodons. The vultures must be waiting for one of them to stumble into the tar.

There's a rustling noise behind you. You turn and stare in horror. You had been so intent on watching the animals half a mile away that you did not hear *this* creature creeping up on you. It's built rather like a tiger, but it's far bigger than any tiger you have ever seen. It has no stripes and its tail is short, but the most remarkable thing about it is its teeth. Two great fangs reach downward from its upper jaw. This is no ordinary tiger. This is a saber-toothed cat!

The cat lowers its powerful neck and growls at you. Its jaws open to an incredible gape, its lips curl back, and its eyes close to slits.

You're starting to panic. What can you do? Turn and run, or stand still and hope the saber-tooth leaves you alone?

 Run! Turn to page 66.

 Stand still. Turn to page 42.

ou are standing in a long corridor with rooms opening on each side. Walking along the corridor in both directions are great numbers of young people carrying books and papers. You have arrived in a college somewhere, and classes are letting out.

Through the window in the door beside you, you can see a class still in session. The lecturer is standing in front of a blackboard covered in graphs headed "Ice Age." You decide that this may be interesting and slip in quietly to the back of the class. The lecturer is just winding up the lesson.

"Now," she says. "Remembering what I have just been talking about, how many advances of the ice were there in the Pleistocene Ice Age?"

"Four main ones," replies one girl. "And maybe about twenty smaller fluctuations."

"Correct. And what happens to the sea level when the ice advances?"

"It goes down because of all the water locked up in the ice."

"Right. When a lowering of sea level exposes land bridges from one continent to another animals can migrate across them. What are good examples of this?"

Another student answers. "Beringia—the land bridge that used to join Asia and North America. Bison, horses, and reindeer used to migrate freely from one to another during the Ice Age."

Bison, horses, and reindeer? That sounds like a familiar collection of animals. Of course You realize that those are the animals that appear on the cave wall with the unicorn.

"There's another bridge between North and South America," says another student. "But that one wasn't really affected by the rise and fall of sea level. It was mountain-building processes that threw that one up near the beginning of the Ice Age.

"Africa used to be joined to Europe as well, and so did the islands of the Mediterranean. It was the rise and fall in sea level that joined and separated them."

"Correct," says the lecturer. "Many animals that *Homo sapiens* hunted became extinct about ten thousand years ago. Which were they?"

"Mammoths," says one student.

"Mastodons," says another.

"Cave bears."

"Woolly rhinoceroses."

"Irish elk."

"Unicorns." You said it without thinking!

The rest of the class turns to look at you and starts laughing. You feel ridiculous. What made you say that? You have never felt so embarrassed in all your life. You must find a quiet corner and jump away—as far as you can.

You could go to Africa in early times, to see what animals there were there. Or you could go to Beringia at the height of the Ice Age and try to watch the animals migrating.

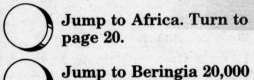

Jump to Africa. Turn to page 20.

Jump to Beringia 20,000 years ago. Turn to page 31.

ou are on the same grassy plain, but the climate is warmer. You're at the beginning of the Pleistocene Epoch, 1.6 million years B.P.

The horses are gone, and so are the mastodons. The giant ground sloths are still there, as well as some other things that you can't quite make out. You climb up on a rounded boulder to gain a better view of the indistinguishable humps in the grass.

Now you can see that they are armadillos. But they are as big as cars: they're called *Glyptodon.*

The boulder beneath your feet lurches. You lose your footing and tumble off, falling face first in the dusty soil. You look round to see what caused this strange tremor—and to your amazement, a door swings up in the front of the rock. Beneath it is a head with a pair of great cowlike eyes. The boulder itself was a *Glyptodon* curled up in its defense position.

These are all typically South American animals. The North American forms are missing. You must have come to a time before the land

bridge of Central America was established. There is no mixing of animal types.

And no spotted horned beast. Time to check out other early Pleistocene continents.

 Jump to Africa. Turn to page 20.

Jump to the west. Turn to page 61.

You leap back into the cave. The bear is still there. Momentarily dazzled by the beam of your flashlight, it rears up, towering above you to twice your height. What made you think you could defeat such a powerful animal as this?

The bear swings at you with one of its great paws. You duck, and save your head. But a second swing catches you on the shoulder and you go sprawling among the bones again. You leap to your feet, snatching a long limb bone from the soil of the cave floor. You shout, to try to distract the monster, and as your shout goes echoing down the cave, you swing the bone around your head and land it with a *whack!* on its nose.

The bear drops to all fours and backs off. Pressing your advantage, you run forward and hit it with the bone again. With a growl it lunges back at you, then rears up once more. The great paws close around you. You feel the beginnings of the crushing hug that will grind your bones and squeeze the life out of your pulp. You must get away from this!

 Jump! Turn to page 4.

Again you are standing on a grassy plain. You wanted to go to Australia, but the landscape looks like North and South America, which you just left. You wonder if you've made a mistake.

Suddenly you notice a large animal rearing above the grasses. Now you know you've come to the wrong place. It's *another* giant ground sloth!

You move closer for a better look. This sloth is quite different from the giant ground sloths you have seen before. Its ears are longer and its coat is shorter. Suddenly you tread on the tip of a long tail. The sloth looks around, startled. It takes fright and goes leaping away.

Now you see that it's not a giant ground sloth at all. It is a kangaroo—nearly ten feet tall! It has a much shorter face and a shorter tail than any kangaroo you have ever seen, but now you know that you are in Australia after all. *Procoptodon* is its name.

You hear a terrible screeching and snarling noise. You look up to see the great shape of the kangaroo, stopped in its tracks and heaving itself up and down. A striped wolflike creature has sunk its fangs into the kangaroo's throat and is hanging on. The kangaroo tries to break away, but its attacker is holding fast and kicking and scratching at its belly with its claws. There is a numbing shriek from the kangaroo. Blood spurts from its throat, and the great animal keels over into the grass.

Now you see its attacker clearly. It is a *Thylacynus*. In Australia, a continent separated from all the others, animal life has gone its own way. Nearly all the mammals here are marsupials—that is, they carry their immature young in a pouch instead of giving birth to them fully developed. The marsupials evolved into forms that look almost exactly the same as the more familiar mammals in the rest of the world. *Thylacynus* is a marsupial wolf.

And this one has brought down and killed the giant kangaroo. The drama does not end there, however. You hear a barking and yelping noise. Several yellowish forms have burst from the thick grasses and are driving the wolf away from its kill. These creatures are true dogs—dingoes. This means that by this time, 20,000 years before our present day, people have landed somewhere on the continent. They have brought dogs with them, and these have run wild and become the dingoes. You realize that this is why the *Thylacynus* is doomed to extinction: dingoes can hunt more efficiently and can compete for its food.

The *Thylacynus* before you is now frantic with hunger, having lost its prey to these newcomers. It needs meat now! It smells you. It stalks toward you through the grass, long mouth slobbering.

No way are you staying to fight such a thing. You turn and run, hampered by the grass and weighed down by your backpack. You are not making much progress, and the striped form circles round you and leaps for your throat.

You twist frantically out of the way—and the corner of your pack catches the side of the animal's head. Its leap is broken, and it falls heavily on its side in the grass. Catlike, it's up and ready for another attack in a moment. You bring around your backpack and hold it in front of you like a shield, but you realize that you can't hope to defeat a creature like this. You had better go!

 Jump! Turn to page 62.

You're standing in a forest amid a herd of elephants that only come as high as your waist! Startled by your sudden appearance, they turn and scamper off into the undergrowth.

Did you really see that, you wonder? Elephants? No bigger than pigs?

You push through the trees to follow them, just to make sure your eyes are not playing tricks on you. The elephants seem to have vanished completely, but you do come across a hippopotamus that's no bigger than the elephants. You wonder what the size of the animals says about the climate. Or is there some other reason for the existence of these dwarf creatures?

The hippopotamus bounds off, frightened by something in the undergrowth. You look around, and your eyes open in horror. Rats! As big as dogs! What kind of nightmare place is this?

As the rats sweep down upon you, you jump for a low branch and swing yourself into a tree. You're safe for the moment while the hideous creatures mill about below.

60

Is this a good place to look for your unicorn? you wonder. Certainly not. You can think of two reasons why these animals are so strange. The first is that you are on an island, probably in the Mediterranean, where the rise and fall of sea level has marooned the animal life, which is developing its own forms. The second is that you are too far back in time for animals to have developed modern types. In either case, early man never painted anything like these!

 Jump to the north to reach mainland Europe. Turn to page 108.

 Jump forward in time. Turn to page 92.

You're standing on a white coral beach. Coconut palms are waving all around you. It is a low tropical island in the middle of the Pacific at the beginning of the Pleistocene. Offshore the coral reef stretches out for several hundred yards to where you can see the Pacific breakers plunging and spraying in the bright sunlight.

This isn't the kind of place you usually associate with an ice age. It is a beautiful, peaceful spot. You feel that, after all the dangers you have been through, you could relax here for a long time. Unfortunately, that would not help you in your quest.

 Jump to Australia. Turn to page 54.

 Jump to North America. Turn to page 36.

ou are in Australia, 20,000 years before the present day. You're standing on a perfectly flat expanse of white crystalline substance: a layer of salt on a dried-up lake bed.

Not far away a cloud of white dust is being kicked up by a chase. A large animal about the size of a rhinoceros is being chased by four or five humans. As they come closer you can see that the animal is a *Diprotodon*—a gigantic wombat. The men are trying to bring it down with *boomerangs*—bent sticks that spin when they're thrown.

The great bearlike shape races toward you across the dazzling surface. Suddenly it sees you and tries to dodge off in a different direction. The ground beneath you shivers, and with a crunching noise it crumbles into a dark hole beneath the charging animal. Uttering an echoing bellow, the marsupial disappears with a splash into the murky fluid below and is gone. The lake bed isn't completely dried up, and the crust of salt is too thin to take much weight.

The hunters halt in their charge, confused. However, one runs on, heedless of the danger. With a crunch he too breaks through the brittle crust. As he sinks into the black brine he throws himself forward spread-eagle and lies facedown on the salt. He has gone through up to his waist, and now he doesn't dare move for fear of breaking through completely. His companions stand back, afraid. Their weight would also be too much for the crust.

Only you are in a position to help. You are much smaller than they are, and the salt may take your weight.

You shake off your backpack and lie facedown. Then slowly, carefully, you creep across the stinging salt toward the trapped man. As you approach him you pick up one of the boomerangs and hold it out toward him. He reaches out and grabs it. Then you feel hands at your ankles. The other members of the hunting party have crept out over the salt after you and have now caught you by the feet. They are pulling you back, and pulling their companion out at the same time.

The rescue is a success!

Later, back at their camp, you're being feasted. You keep your eyes closed and pretend that you are eating fried chicken instead of slivers of lizard roasted over the fire and fat grubs cooked alive in the embers. You know that you are being honored by being invited to share the sparse meal, and you don't want to appear rude by not enjoying it.

The party consists of men only. Presumably they are on a long trek away from their permanent home to look for food. The men are built like modern-day humans. They must be the ancestors of today's Australian aborigines.

The climate is not as hot as you would expect for Australia. In the northern hemisphere the Ice Age will be in full rage, but here, in the tropics, the climate is merely cooler than normal. That would explain the giant animals you have seen. Larger animals develop in cooler climates because their big bodies keep in the heat better.

This thought brings you back to what you're doing here—looking for a unicorn or whatever the creature is.

You call to the man that you rescued, and with a stick you draw the unicorn shape in the soil. The man jumps up and down, pointing excitedly to a rocky ridge that towers about a mile away from the camp. He walks briskly off toward it, beckoning you to follow.

Your excitement mounts. As you coming close to the end of your quest? Are you going to find your mystery animal here in Australia? He takes you to a spot beneath an overhanging rock and points proudly to the wall.

Rock paintings! But nothing like the ones you are looking for. These paintings are mostly of lizards, kangaroos, and people. There are no paintings of horses, deer, or buffalo—and no unicorn beast. You know now that you are on the wrong continent altogether.

You are in the wrong time as well. Here the paintings are quite well developed, so you need to be further back in time. You have not yet explored Europe thoroughly. You could try there.

Jump to Europe 40,000 years B.P. Turn to page 58.

You turn and flee, wondering how quickly saber-tooths can run. Then you get an idea. The saber-tooth is a cat, and cats don't like water. You turn and plunge into a nearby pond and begin wading out to the middle.

But suddenly your feet sink into a gooey layer beneath the water. You're trapped. You have blundered into a tar pit—just like thousands of other Ice Age animals!

Your struggling tips you over, and you fall full-length in the knee-deep water. You fling out a hand to save yourself—and it sinks into the tar and sticks fast. Then you remember the saber-tooth! You look around frantically. But the tiger has forgotten you. It's off in the distance stalking the mastodon herd. Saber-toothed cats are only equipped to kill big elephantine animals. It would not have been interested in you.

Something else is interested in you, though. With a *caw!* a great vulture lifts into the air from a nearby tree, spirals upward, and glides down toward you.

You're completely vulnerable, trapped up to your neck in water with only one hand free. You swing your fist at the great vulture as it dives, and it swerves to the side. But it's far bigger than any vulture you have ever seen, and a waving fist is not going to distract it for long.

The huge bird swoops again. You'd better get away from here.

Jump to Alaska. Turn to page 36.

Jump to the Rocky Mountains. Turn to page 100.

ou try to get into a better position to hear what's being said.

Suddenly one of the young men looks up, sees your face pressed against the porthole, and gives a startled shout.

You pull your face away. "Hey!" comes a voice from behind you. You turn. A sailor is coming at you.

"Come here!" he shouts. "You're a stowaway!"

"No, I'm not," you shout, backing away around the corner of the cabin.

You turn to run and hide, but you catch your foot on a cable attached to some sampling equipment and fall heavily onto the deck. Footsteps sound behind you. You scramble quickly to your feet.

Just at that moment the ship gives a lurch as a sudden swell catches it. You lose your balance, tumble over the gunwale, and plunge into the sea. Water closes over you, cutting out the sounds of shouting from the deck. You'd better do something quick before you pass out altogether.

Jump back 20,000 years. Turn to page 36.

Jump to dry land. Turn to page 108.

You slip and tumble down a grassy slope, the smell of crushed alpine flowers all around you. Vaguely you are aware of towering snow-capped peaks and a deep green valley below into which you are falling. Suddenly your perilous slide down the steep bank ends as you slither into a group of figures and fetch up against a pile of bones by a fire.

About a dozen people are staring at you in amazement. They're different from any you have seen so far. They are definitely human, but their necks are short and their heads low, with protruding jaws and eyebrows and broad, flat noses. They must be *Homo sapiens neanderthalensis* —Neanderthal man!

You recover from the shock before they do. "Hello," you say. "Can I join you for supper?"

This spurs them into action. A fur-clad arm is thrown around your throat from behind,·and another pins your arms to your sides. Not much of a welcome for a stranger! Then, for the first time, you notice what kind of bones lie by the fire. Human bones! Broken to extract the marrow, and a human skull with the top smashed in and the brain scooped out. It looks as if these people may have you for supper after all. They are cannibals!

A wave of nausea sweeps over you. You try to squirm free, but it's no use—your captors are too strong for you. One man, taller than the rest but still not much taller than you, approaches you with a stone knife.

You hear a yell from one of the cannibals. With a roar a cave bear lumbers into the group, rears up, and, with a swing of its mighty paw, breaks the neck of the man with the knife. You are dropped to the ground as the cannibals panic and scramble for weapons.

You run for your life along the hillside. You want to get as far away as possible from that horrible place. You cast a look behind and see that the bear is being defeated by the overwhelming number of Neanderthals. But then you stumble and go headlong into the mouth of a cave. You feel your head strike a rock, and blackness bursts all around you.

When you come to, you are cold and weak. You must have been out for hours, for it's early evening now. The valley below the cave is dark, and the snowy slopes opposite are tinged with sunset red.

You have no intention of staying here near those savages, but you can't go anywhere else!

In the struggle, you dropped your backpack and all your equipment back at the fire.

You can't see far into the cave, but there seem to be several cave bear skulls lying there. What would be worse? Facing the cave bears or facing the cannibals?

Then you hear a kind of chanting. You look out of the cave and see a little procession approaching. Four of the Neanderthal men, carrying torches, are grouped around a fifth who is clutching something precious to his chest. They are approaching the cave. You step back into the darkness—and knock something over. As the procession reaches the mouth of the cave, you hide yourself deep in the shadows. By the light of their torches you see now that the floor is not littered with bear bones: Instead, each of the skulls has been put on a kind of pedestal of stones.

The men stop by the bear skull that you have just sent flying from its perch and reverently replace it. Next they walk over to the opposite wall. The torchlight flickers on the item that they have just brought. It is a fresh bear skull—probably from the animal that attacked the camp. As you watch, they place it in a niche in the wall and then step back. The man who placed it there raises his arms and begins a chant.

With a thrill you realize that you have stumbled on an early form of religious belief.

They must worship the strength and courage of the cave bear, and this place must be some kind of shrine. And the skulls on their pedestals and in their niches are the symbols of this belief.

You slip quietly out of the cave and into the gathering dusk. You must collect your belongings and be gone from this place.

As you leave, you notice another group holding torches. Making your way across to them, you see that they are burying the man who was killed by the bear. His body lies in a shallow pit, on a bed of pine boughs and flowers, surrounded by stone tools. The men and women stand around in the torchlight chanting. The chant is different from that uttered by the men in the bear cave—sadder and more wistful.

This is very strange. These people revere the cave bear. They bury their dead with dignity. But they eat strangers! The cannibalism can't have anything to do with a shortage of food. There's plenty of game around. Maybe they believe that by consuming their enemies they absorb the enemies' strength.

People seem to be developing these rituals in order to relate to the big, dangerous world about them.

Silently you creep back to the fire in the deserted camp and gather your belongings. Where should you go now? Should you jump somewhere else at this time to see if Neanderthal men hunt your mystery animal? Or should you jump forward and meet more advanced people?

Jump somewhere else in this time period. Turn to page 115.

Jump forward 20,000 years. Turn to page 90.

A wall of quivering gray flesh rises above you and rolls toward you. You back away from it, stones crunching beneath your boots, and collide with another blubbery mass behind you. At first you think that these things are elephants, but you can't see any legs. Anyway, you want to get away from them before they crush you.

You run, and find yourself at the edge of the sea—cold gray waves breaking on a stony beach. You can see the animals now. There are six of them, and they seem to be huge seals—forty feet long! You recognize them as Steller's sea cows, huge mountains of flesh and blubber that were hunted to extinction only about 200 years before your own time.

Then, above the crash and roar of the waves, you hear people shouting. Kayaks are being pulled up the beach at the other side of the sea cow herd. A dozen fur-swaddled men wielding harpoons rush toward the nearest sea cow. Before it can escape, they start stabbing it and hacking it with knives. The other animals panic and lumber for the water, rolls of blubber flopping along their massive bodies. They plunge into the sea, heading for safety.

You know better than to interfere with these people in their hunting. You're going to slip away from here unnoticed, but not before you find out more about where you are and see if you are any nearer your goal.

While everybody is occupied cutting up the sea cow that has just been killed, you make a quick dash along the edge of the water to where the kayaks are drawn up. If you could take one of them without being noticed, you might be able to reach their camp. You throw your backpack into the narrow cockpit of one of the skin boats and push it out into the waves. Then you jump in, seize the paddle, and start paddling.

"Hey!" comes a shout. You have been seen.

You look behind you. Two men have broken away from the hunting party and are running down to the boats. They climb into a two-man kayak and paddle out after you. Now you're in trouble! They are faster and more experienced than you. They'll catch up soon.

But luck is on your side. Their kayak is suddenly thrown into the air as a sea cow surfaces like an island beneath them. The great animal hardly notices what it has done; it just paddles on. The two men struggle for the shore, where their companions pull them out.

You paddle along, parallel to the shore, and soon you see a settlement. It's made of dome-shaped turf huts. Fires burn here and there, and other kayaks are drawn up on the beach.

This is still Beringia, but these people seem to be quite different from the ones you saw here last. The people you saw 10,000 years ago must have been the ancestors of the Indians migrating to America from Asia. These people must be the ancestors of the Inuit—the people we call the Eskimo. As you approach, you can see several women around the fires, making animal-skin clothing.

But you don't think that you are any nearer your goal. The tundra landscape that stretches to the horizon beyond the encampment does not seem to have any animal life at all. No horses, no buffalo, and certainly no unicorns. You should be a good deal farther south.

Jump to South America.
Turn to page 94.

Darkness! You are in a cave again. You move swiftly to the glow of light that indicates the opening. You have no intention of being faced with a cave bear again.

You reach the entrance and see a wooded gorge below you. You are in the valley of the Dordogne River in central France. In a hollow in the limestone cliff, near its base, a group of people are skinning a huge deer with a spread of antlers ten feet across. Humans—modern humans again—have moved in and made this rock shelter their home. A barrier of poles and skins provides a wall, and a fire burns on the stone hearth.

Suddenly one of the men who was cutting up the deer picks up a stick coated with what looks like animal fat and plunges its end into the fire. It takes light and burns like a torch. He climbs with it up the cliff face toward you.

You are alarmed. Maybe you shouldn't be here. You duck back into the cave before you are seen.

You are out of luck. The man was coming

into the cave anyway. You retreat farther from the entrance, hoping that the darkness will hide you. Then you notice it! The walls are covered with engravings. Not paintings, but engravings. Figures of animals are scratched into the walls everywhere.

The man stops and puts down his torch. He lifts a stone from the floor and begins, patiently, to draw the shape of the huge deer on the wall.

Cave art at last! This is more like it! The animal engravings are much simpler than the paintings you are looking for. They are drawn with one leg representing the forelegs, and one representing the hind. You must have come to a time that's earlier than the culture that produced the unicorn and the other animals.

You are so excited that you forget yourself and utter a happy little chuckle. The artist halts in his work and looks around, startled. He shouts at you and shakes his torch. He's angry that this sacred place is being violated.

Time to go again! You retreat farther into the cave before you jump.

 Jump forward in time. Turn to page 87.

A spear whistles by close to your ear and thuds into the flank of a deer standing close to you. You have jumped from the middle of one hunt to the middle of another! The deer, in its death agony, leaps and twists. The protruding spear catches you on the leg and sends you sprawling in the long grass.

A group of Neanderthal men and boys run up to finish off their kill and to take it away. Two of them crouch down next to you and feel you all over to see if you are hurt. Luckily nothing is broken, but you'll have a beautiful bruise on the thigh before long. The two men help you to your feet, supporting you between them, and you join the group as it marches off across the plain, dragging the dead deer along.

This is a lot better than your other meetings with the Neanderthals. At least these people do not seem to have cannibalism on their minds!

The group climbs up over a rise, and before you stands another band. This party, also of men and boys, is different. They are clad in the same sort of furs and carry similar weapons; however, they are taller than the Neanderthals and have longer faces.

You are looking at modern men, *Homo sapiens sapiens,* the first you have seen in ancient Europe. These modern men—called Cro-Magnon, after a site in France where their remains were found—replaced the Neanderthals in central Europe at about this time. You brace yourself for a battle.

Instead the two groups stand, wave their spears, and shout at one another. Then you are pushed forward, prodded from behind by a spear, and the Neanderthals climb down, without a battle.

That is it! The Neanderthals recognize you as belonging more to the Cro-Magnon group than to themselves, and they're handing you over! The two societies must be on quite friendly terms.

Then you notice something odd. Some of the Cro-Magnon have the heavy eyebrows of the Neanderthal. The two groups must be able to interbreed. Perhaps the Neanderthal did not die out. Perhaps they were just absorbed into the Cro-Magnon population.

The Cro-Magnon group look at you curiously. They don't seem to want to accept you either, so they turn and leave you standing there. The Neanderthals have already gone. You are alone.

Now what will you do? You could follow this

Cro-Magnon group to see if they show the same artistic development as the Neanderthals. Or you could jump forward several thousand years to see how their culture advances.

 Follow the group. Turn to page 111.

 Jump forward 15,000 years. Turn to page 90.

Again it is dark. You have landed in another cave! If this goes on, you'll need light of your own. You reach into your backpack for a flashlight and switch it on.

What a sight meets your eyes!

Bulls, horses, reindeer—all around you on the cave walls. Brightly painted in reds, blacks, browns, and whites. The animals are so realistically drawn that you can almost see them running, jumping, wading a river.

You know you have arrived! This is the very cave and there is the very unicorn painting that you are investigating! But you have jumped too far forward in time. The cave has obviously been deserted and sealed for years.

You can hear a scrabbling and scraping noise. You put out your light. Light bursts in at one corner, and two young boys not much older than you scramble into the cave. They are carrying lanterns, and you hope that you are not caught in their glow. Suddenly the light falls on one of the paintings.

There is a cry from the boy behind the torch. "Marcel!" he yells excitedly. "Look at this!"

The year is 1940. You must have come into

the cave at the moment of its discovery! You stay in the darkness to listen to the excited discoverers.

"Prehistoric people must have made these," whispers one boy in awe.

"We'll have to tell the Abbé Breuil about this," says the other.

"Yes, the priest knows all about the other cave paintings around here. I bet he doesn't know anything about *this!*"

The two go scrambling back to the entrance.

"Wait a minute!" says the first. "What are we going to say we were doing here? We can't tell anybody about the prank we were going to play."

"We'll just say that we were trying to rescue our dog—that he'd fallen down a hole. That should keep us out of trouble!"

As the boys disappear you wonder vaguely what they were really up to. But that doesn't matter. What does matter is that you have found the painting you are looking for, here in a cave in central France—but you are still no nearer to finding out what the mysterious creature is.

You could try jumping forward in time to see if later studies shed any light on it.

Jump forward. Turn to page 102.

You are back on tundra plains. There is a scattering of birch forest beneath the gray sky. Snow powders the ground, and there is a blue chill everywhere as a cold winter's evening draws on. It's 20,000 years before the present day in what is now Russia.

Beyond a stand of birch there is a herd of woolly elephants. These are taller than the mastodon you saw in America. Their heads are held way above the ground, and their backs slope down to the hips. Their tusks are long and curving and their shoulders are humped. You recognize these as mammoths.

A great trumpeting noise sounds from one side. You push your way through the scrubby trees, sparkling and heavy with frost, to see what is happening. A huge bull mammoth is trapped in a peat bog. It's struggling to free itself, but it only succeeds in sinking deeper.

Then you notice that you are not the only observer. A group of men—modern-type men—are watching from the edge of the birch thicket. A pair of them carry a huge slab of meat slung on a pole between their shoulders. They've already caught their mammoth; they're not really interested in this new source of meat. Their leader, a tall man with a gray beard, signals impatiently, and the hunters turn and walk away.

You wonder what to do next. You could follow the hunters and see what kind of people they are. But you can't help feeling sorry for the trapped mammoth. Should you wait and see if it escapes?

 Follow the hunters. Turn to page 96.

 Watch the mammoth. Turn to page 107.

You're standing on the steel deck of a ship on the open ocean. It's evening and the sea is calm. Along the deck are arranged all sorts of sampling instruments, evidently designed to take specimens from the ocean floor and bring them back. You see dredges, grabs, and core samplers. This must be some sort of oceanographic vessel.

Lights are on in a cabin in the ship's stern. You steal along the gently moving deck to see what's happening. Through an open porthole you can see several men and women relaxing over coffee, and you can hear them talking about their work.

"That was a beautiful core sample we got this afternoon," says one man.

"Yes," says a girl sitting next to him. "It was a marvelous cross section of the ocean-bottom mud here. You could see cold-water mud, on and on for about twenty cycles. You could see right away that the ice of the Ice Age had come and gone at least twenty times."

"We can start checking the fossils in it tomorrow," remarks another man. "Pity we need microscopes to find fossils in a core sample. It would be easier if they were all like that." He waves his coffee cup at something just out of sight from you. You change your position and see that he's pointing to a huge set of antlers hanging on the bulkhead. "Where did that come from, Jack?"

The older man, who had spoken first, replies, "Off Denmark. We dredged it up last year. It dates from a time where the sea level was so low that there was dry land from Europe to Britain."

This could be something of a clue, you think. Deer like that are supposed to appear on the same cave paintings as your unicorn beast. You could follow that up in Ice Age Europe.

Stay and eavesdrop some more. Turn to page 69.

Jump to Europe 40,000 years ago. Turn to page 108.

You are in the darkness of a cave, a zoo smell of huge animals all around you. Dimly you can make out the elephantine forms of three huge shaggy animals in the cave with you. Trying not to disturb them, you make for the dazzling triangle that is the cave mouth. You scramble onto a wall of boulders that is blocking off the cave entrance and look out over the bright landscape.

You are in the foothills of a great mountain range. The air is clear and crisp. A herd of horses grazes in the distance, and a pair of mastodons—shaggy elephants with long low profiles—snatch leaves and twigs from a tree on the slope below you.

Then you notice the stones that you are standing on. They form a wall across the opening of the cave, and they have been placed there for a reason. Why? And by whom?

You look back into the cave. The animals that you first saw are giant ground sloths—huge, shaggy animals with little heads, heavy bowed limbs, and big curving claws. And they have been penned up here deliberately. This is a good sign, because it suggests the work of human beings. People must have spread out from Beringia, down through North America, across the Central American land bridge, and into South America. And they've been here long enough to settle down. They're even practicing a kind of animal farming, keeping next week's dinner safely locked up.

"Ho!"

You whip around. A man is coming up the slope at you, waving a spear.

"Ho!" the man shouts again.

Suddenly you feel guilty and vulnerable, as if you had been caught on an orchard fence, about to steal apples. How can you explain to this man that you are not trying to rustle his giant ground sloths?

You don't have to. You miss your footing on the uneven boulders and tumble into the cave—rolling right into the midst of the sloths. They rear up on their giant hind legs and tails. The huge up-curved claws are perilously close to your head. You'd better jump out of here before you're trampled. But where to?

Jump back to the beginning of the Pleistocene. Turn to page 50.

Jump back 10,000 years to Europe. Turn to page 4.

The hunting party is joined by others. All of them are weighed down by meat. Some men carry mammoth tusks over their shoulders. They are all heading toward a clump of huts across the plain. Tall streamers of smoke rise into the chill evening stillness from this encampment, and the glow of fires is a welcoming sight.

As you tag along unnoticed at the rear of Graybeard's party, you notice that the huts are dome-shaped. They are made of skins stretched on a loose curving framework of poles and weighed down at the edges by mammoth skulls and tusks. The whole place has a rather temporary air about it.

These people, you realize, must be nomads. It looks as if they get everything they need from the mammoths. They probably follow the mammoth herds in their migrations and set up camp in their feeding grounds. This must be one of the first steps toward the domestication of animals!

You're able to walk around freely in the encampment. In the evening gloom your hooded

parka and boots are easily mistaken for the animal skin clothing worn by everyone else here.

Your foot kicks something heavy along the ground. You bend down to pick it up. It's a piece of ivory as big as your fist—the tip of a mammoth tusk. It could make you rich in your own time, but here this precious substance is so common that they build houses out of it!

By the light of a fire, where some women are cooking great chunks of mammoth meat, you see an old man working a handful of clay into a figure. You walk over and sit down beside him. He doesn't seem to object to you watching him. The figure he is working on looks like the figure of a woman, but very fat and with the legs tapering away to points instead of feet.

He looks up at you, and then at the piece of ivory in your hand. He stretches out his hand for it, and you give it to him. He puts aside his figure, picks up a stone tool with a fine point, and begins to engrave a picture of a mammoth on the ivory.

Here, you realize, is the beginning of representational art—pictures that actually look like something. Now you're really getting somewhere! You're on the right track with the subject matter, too. Mammoth paintings are found near your unicorn painting.

This is art, but not cave art. You're unlikely

to find caves here on the steppes of ancient Russia. Try the more mountainous areas of central Europe.

 Jump to the west. Turn to page 80.

You are perched on a crag in the Rocky Mountains. Down below you is a valley glacier, quite different from the broad ice sheets you have seen so far. You can see how the ice surface is puckered and cracked into crevasses as it creeps gradually around the curves of its course. Long slabs of material blemish the glittering white surface as the rocks of the valley sides are crushed and carried away.

The sight is so beautiful that you want to shout with joy at being alone with all this splendor. A yodel seems appropriate.

"Yodellodellodelleiiii!" you burst out at the top of your voice. The echo carries back from the opposite wall and is repeated up the valley.

As it dies away you hear another noise. A rumbling noise. You look around you. The wall of snow behind you is collapsing in a smoky chaos and sweeping down the hill. Your shout has started an avalanche, and it's hurtling toward you!

You don't know how to save yourself. You can't run to the side because the crags are too steep. Away down the slope, almost at the glacier's edge, there stands a grove of pine trees. If you could reach them, they might check the fury of the avalanche.

You leap down from your ledge onto the snow slope below and run headlong. Luckily the snow is not too deep, and you can run in it. You let one foot fall in front of the other as you allow gravity to pull you down the precipitous slope. Now you have almost reached the first of the trees. The roar of the avalanche is deafening, and it is joined by the snapping noise of shattered timber. Darkness floods over you as you are engulfed, icy snow penetrating every seam in your clothing, and you are carried away.

You must get out of this!

 Turn to page 36.

You are still in the cave, but it's light now, and you're surrounded by people. They are tourists of every nationality, and they're being shown the wall paintings. Their guide is a man whom you recognize as Marcel, one of the boys who discovered the paintings in 1940.

"Ladies and gentlemen," he says, "welcome to the cave of Lascaux. Here is the greatest example of Paleolithic art in the world. Here are pictures of the animals that Ice Age men hunted—painted 15,000 years ago. They were discovered twenty years ago when a dog fell down a hole."

"Havers!" you exclaim to yourself.

You tag along with the party until at last you see the mystery figure on the wall. It's just like the illustrations you have seen—a large, spotted animal with a single horn. Of course, Marcel has no idea what it is supposed to be.

If you go forward in time you may come across someone who has done some research on it and can tell you what it is. You leave the party and move into a quiet corner from where you can jump.

 Jump forward. Turn to page 106.

ou stand, shivering in soaking clothes, on the banks of a river that flows through a cold, gloomy pine forest. Beside you, on a stony bank, is a tent. Two hobbled horses stand beyond, quietly grazing. A pack of sleigh dogs are chewing some chunks of meat nearby.

"He-elp!" you shout through chattering teeth. If you do not find warmth soon, you will perish.

You are in luck! A fur-hatted head pops out of the tent flap. "Ivan!" he shouts. "There is someone out here. Fetch a blanket." Another man, dressed in a heavy coat and big boots, rushes out with a blanket and puts it around you. The two of them lead you into the warmth of the tent.

"Why are you wet? Where have you come from?" he asks. "Who are you? What are you doing here?"

You cannot answer him, your teeth are chattering so much. And even if you could, how would you explain? You avoid their eyes as you pretend to faint from exhaustion. You collapse into a pile of furs near the warm fire. After a minute, you hear the men leave the tent.

You look out through the flap of the tent—and you see something you didn't notice before. There are several mammoth tusks stacked outside. Where did they come from? These are modern times, judging by the oil lamps and the rifles in the tent.

But the warmth of the oil stove makes you sleepy . . .

You must have fallen asleep. You shake yourself awake and look out of the tent flap. A very strange sight meets your eyes.

Protruding from the frozen soil of the river bank is the carcass of a mammoth, buried and frozen many thousands of years ago. Your two rescuers are hacking away at the skull, trying to remove the tusks. Every now and again one of them hacks off a piece of flesh from the trunk and tosses it to the dogs.

So that is what these people are doing! They're harvesting the valuable ivory from mammoth corpses frozen in the tundra mud. You'd like to tell them to stop—to explain that these fossils would be of more value to science and humankind if left intact.

But after all, you are in their country and it is their job. And you don't feel that you can argue with people who have just saved your life! You'd better leave them to it and get back on the trail.

 Jump. Turn to page 108.

Darkness again. You are still in Lascaux, but you are alone. The tourists are long gone. You shine your light on the walls. The paintings are still there—but what has happened to them?

They are faded to pale remains of their former beauty. A green growth is spreading over some of them.

This is what happened in twenty years of tourism. The paintings stood unchanged and undisturbed for 15,000 years. Then suddenly thousands of visitors trooped through—breathing, changing the atmosphere, changing the temperature—and the paintings have begun to fade away.

Nobody comes here now. It has been all locked up and sealed since 1963. You know that you should not be here either. You must go.

You could go somewhere else at the present day and see what other research is being done. You now know that the pictures were painted 15,000 years ago in Lascaux. You could go back to that time.

 Jump somewhere else at the present day. Turn to page 92.

 Jump back 15,000 years. Turn to page 118.

ou let the hunters march off, and you try to get closer to the stricken mammoth. It sinks visibly into the icy mud as it thrashes desperately.

Suddenly there is a crackle of crushed ice from the mud below your feet. You've broken through the thin frozen crust! Bitterly cold peat oozes over your boots and up to your knees. You reach out frantically and grab a tussock of fragile yellow grass stems, but the fluid is up to your waist now. Talk about clutching at straws! You are sharing the fate of the trapped mammoth.

Not if you can help it!

Jump safely to modern times. Turn to page 103.

arkness surrounds you. The air is cold but stuffy and close at the same time. You fumble for your flashlight and illuminate a damp rock wall. You're in a cave. This is more like it, you think to yourself. The paintings you are trying to decipher are found in caves.

You hear a snuffling noise behind you. You turn, and the beam of your flashlight shows a great mass of fur. It's a bear, roused from its hibernation by your sudden arrival. And it is huge! Far larger than any grizzly bear you have seen.

Dimly you are aware of other sleeping bears behind it, but you have little time to appreciate the details. The bear you woke up seems very angry.

You turn and run. A chill wind is blowing down the passage. You run in that direction, hoping that it leads to the open air. Your foot catches in something hard and jagged embedded in the floor, and you fall with a crash. There, in front of your eyes, the bared teeth and hollow eyes of a skull leer at you.

Without pausing to think, you snatch the skull out of the soil and hurl it at the approaching bear, hitting it squarely on the nose. It halts in its charge, giving you time to scramble up and over the mass of bones that you now see cover the floor. You make for the exit. The bones seem to be those of other cave bears. They must have hibernated in this very cave for generation after generation.

Suddenly you find yourself outside in the bitter cold of an Ice Age winter night. The cold is so piercing that your exposed skin becomes numb. You know that you will be frostbitten unless you find shelter immediately. You can run back into the cave and fight the bears for possession. Or you can jump forward into summer.

 Jump to summer. Turn to page 70.

 Return to the cave. Turn to page 53.

You hear a shouting and clattering of sticks from the direction in which the Cro-Magnon party disappeared. You sprint to the top of a rise and look down the next slope.

There, among the tall waving grasses of the cold plain, they have found a woolly rhinoceros grazing. They surround it—jumping, shouting, and beating sticks and spears together to make a noise.

The shaggy beast is terrified by all this din. It waves its heavy head from side to side looking for a way of escape. Then it makes a sudden break in one direction, crashing heavily through the grass and bushes. The men quickly dash forward to head it off. The rhinoceros halts momentarily, then lumbers off in another direction. The men still follow it, coming very close and throwing sticks and stones at it, but darting nimbly aside from the sweep of the great double horn.

You're very impressed with the bravery and the teamwork of these hunters. But you can't see how they intend to kill something as big as a woolly rhinoceros. They aren't using the spears they carry. All they are doing is making a noise and trying to frighten it.

Now they have turned the animal, and it's heading up the rise toward where you are standing. They are letting it run. Obviously, they're driving the beast, and it's going in the direction that they want!

Toward you!

You run to take cover in some light scrub. The thin birch trees won't be much of a barrier against the charging animal, but you're not going to wait there to be trampled.

Suddenly the ground gives way beneath you. You fall with a sickening jolt.

You roll in a heap in loose soil at the bottom of a dark pit, cracking your head against a wooden stake. Dazed, you look around you. You've fallen into a trap which was set for a large animal. So that's what the men were planning! You have slipped in between the poles supporting the loose covering of vegetation that makes the pit invisible from outside.

Half a dozen stakes, almost as tall as you, have been sharpened at the end and set vertically in the soil of the pit bottom. It was a miracle that you didn't impale yourself as you fell! But your relief is short-lived when you remember that this is the very pit to which the hunters are driving the rhinoceros. From up above, you can hear their shouts. You can

also hear the drumming thump of the great feet as the mighty beast thunders toward the trap.

You must jump. But to where? Forward in time to see how these people develop? Or across to western Europe at the same time, to see their development in another area?

The heavy feet pound overhead. With a crash, sticks and grass burst inward and shower down on you. The pit is flooded with dazzling daylight, and the great brown shaggy body hurtles down toward you!

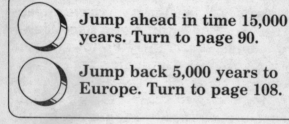

Jump ahead in time 15,000 years. Turn to page 90.

Jump back 5,000 years to Europe. Turn to page 108.

ou are in the Alps, standing on the edge of a deep ravine! Down below there are a number of animal skeletons strewn among the rocks. Moving around them are about a dozen shambling figures. Even from this height you can identify them as Neanderthals, just like those you have already seen. They seem to be waiting for something—they're looking expectantly up toward you. Surely they can't be waiting for you!

You hear shouts and a clattering of rocks from behind you. You turn. A flock of mountain sheep are frantically running down the slope toward the ravine. They are being chased by a group of Neanderthals who are waving sticks and hurling stones.

The sheep are being driven toward a gorge that few can leap. Those that fail will fall to their deaths below and be butchered by the waiting hunters.

Suddenly the whole flock swerves, driven by their instinct for survival. Now they're heading straight for you!

In a few seconds the wave of sheep will hit you and carry you into the ravine! You have no time to think. You must jump!

 Jump forward 5,000 years in time. Turn to page 83.

 Jump to another place. Turn to page 108.

You stand at the entrance to the cave, looking out across the limestone plateau. Some people are moving about among the scattered clumps of birch and pine. They actually seem to be dancing!

You move closer to get a better look. The people are, indeed, dancing. They're dressed in animal skins and furs, just like the earlier people you have seen, but they are all ornamented. They are decorated with strings of beads and bunches of feathers, as though this is a special occasion.

There's music, too. Of a group of about thirty men, women, and children, at least half have some sort of musical instrument—an animal-skin drum, a reed whistle, or just a pair of animal bones that are beaten together.

These people are more advanced than other peoples you have already seen, and you have arrived on some special occasion. This must be a religious celebration—perhaps thanks for a successful hunt or for the coming of spring.

You saw that the Neanderthal had the beginnings of a religion about 25,000 years before this, but they didn't have the art with which to express it. Through your trips in time you've seen art develop from rough clay modeling and scratches on ivory fragments through detailed engravings on cave walls to the magnificent cave paintings of this period. Other arts have obviously developed at the same time.

Now the dance is changing tempo. The music is building up to a more frantic rhythm. The dancers are falling back, making room for one who seems to be taking center stage. He is more gaudily decorated than the rest, with a painted animal skin over his back that covers him from his neck to his knees. He is carrying an object carved from a chunk of wood. As he dances and sways to the clattering, beating music he puts the object over his head, and you see that it is a mask. It is roughly carved as an animal's head, and a pair of shoots that branch off from it have been lashed together and shaped to represent horns. The man now goes down on all fours and hops around, froglike, pretending to be an animal.

You wonder what kind of animal he is supposed to be. The pattern of spots painted on the skin and the shape of the head do seem somehow familiar to you. Then, with a shock, you realize what it is. This is the unicorn figure from the cave!

What can this mean, you wonder? Is the animal on the wall really just some man in a

mask? As you draw closer for another look you see the ritual change. The man takes the mask off and hands it to one of the women. She puts it on, prances around like an animal, and, in turn, hands it on to someone else. Then you are drawn into the group and the mask is placed in your hands. Like the others, you place it over your head and go down on all fours.

It's like wearing a disguise at Halloween: You put on a devil's costume and hide your own face behind a devil's mask, and then you can act just like a devil. You feel the same now. With an animal's mask over your head you act just like an animal. You hop around and grunt, just as an animal would do. In your imagination you actually become an animal!

A young woman pulls the mask from your head and passes it on to someone else. You are left slightly dazed by the experience.

So that is the answer. Early human beings were so dependent on the animal life of this time for food, for clothing, for shelter—that they painted the animals on cave walls and celebrated animal life in dance and mime. Early humans knew that both they and the animals inhabited the same world and showed this by dressing up as animals—actually pretending to be animals—and by sharing the world with them. So that they will remember this for all time, and not just during the festivals, people paint animal figures on the cave walls. That explains the other half-human, half-animal figures that crop up on other cave walls of this period.

You are suddenly saddened that few people in your own twentieth-century civilization think this way. The history of your own people has been one of exploitation. Human beings think they are superior, so they just take what they want from the animal world. The result is the devastation of natural environments and the extinction of species.

At least you have disproved one extinction theory. At the beginning of your quest you thought that there might once have been an animal like a unicorn, an animal that has since died out. Now you can go home and report that the unicorn figure is showing humanity's relationship with the animal life in its world. And if you can help other people to see that that relationship is still important, then so much the better.

MISSION COMPLETED.

DATA FILE

About the Contributors

DOUGAL DIXON is the author of *After Man, A Zoology of the Future,* and *Time Exposure.* He studied Geology and Paleontology at the University of St. Andrews in Scotland and has spent the past ten years in publishing. Many of his articles are included in encyclopedias. He resides in Dorset, England.

DOUG HENDERSON's depictions of the Mesozoic Era have won the admiration of paleontologists and aficionados of natural history art. He has recently completed a children's book with dinosaur expert Jack Horner, and continues to research his favorite subject at the sites of dinosaur digs.

ALEX NINO is an internationally respected illustrator. His work has appeared in such publications as *Metal Hurlant* in France, *Starlog* in America and in hundreds of magazines in his native Philippines. His paintings and illustrations have been published as portfolios, book jackets, and graphic stories. He is also the winner of an Inkpot Award.

Now you can have your favorite Choose Your Own Adventure® Series in a variety of sizes. Along with the popular pocket size, Bantam has introduced the Choose Your Own Adventure® series in a Skylark edition and also in Hardcover.

Now not only do you get to decide on how you want your adventures to end, you also get to decide on what size you'd like to collect them in.

SKYLARK EDITIONS

☐	15309	The Green Slime #6 S. Saunders	$1.95
☐	15195	Help! You're Shrinking #7 E. Packard	$1.95
☐	15201	Indian Trail #8 R. A. Montgomery	$1.95
☐	15190	Dream Trips #9 E. Packard	$1.95
☐	15191	The Genie In the Bottle #10 J. Razzi	$1.95
☐	15222	The Big Foot Mystery #11 L. Sonberg	$1.95
☐	15223	The Creature From Millers Pond #12 S. Saunders	$1.95
☐	15226	Jungle Safari #13 E. Packard	$1.95
☐	15227	The Search For Champ #14 S. Gilligan	$1.95
☐	15241	Three Wishes #15 S. Gilligan	$1.95
☐	15242	Dragons! #16 J. Razzi	$1.95
☐	15261	Wild Horse Country #17 L. Sonberg	$1.95
☐	15262	Summer Camp #18 J. Gitenstein	$1.95
☐	15270	The Tower of London #19 S. Saunders	$1.95
☐	15271	Trouble In Space #20 J. Woodcock	$1.95
☐	15283	Mona Is Missing #21 S. Gilligan	$1.95
☐	15303	The Evil Wizard #22 A. Packard	$1.95
☐	15305	The Flying Carpet #25	$1.95
☐	15318	The Magic Path #26	$1.95
☐	15331	Ice Cave #27	$1.95

Prices and availability subject to change without notice.

Buy them at your local bookstore or use this handy coupon for ordering: